DEPENDENT PERSONALITY *DISORDER*

Your Definitive Guide to Liberation from Dependency

Lilian Nicole

CONTENTS

INTRODUCTION

Individuals suffering from Dependent Personality Disorder frequently struggle with making daily decisions, requiring excessive reassurance, and avoiding responsibilities that might challenge their self-perceived inadequacy.

Dependent personality disorder (DPD) is defined as an inability to be alone and a reliance on others for comfort and support. In comparison with insecurity, which is common, there is a need for reassurance in order to function. It is characterized by a pervasive and excessive desire to be cared for, which leads to submissive and clinging behavior.

For a condition to be labeled as a personality disorder, it must fall into one of the following clusters:

Cluster A: Cluster A personality disorders, which are characterized by unusual or eccentric behavior, include Paranoid, Schizoid, and Schizotypal Personality Disorders. Individuals in this group may exhibit social withdrawal, suspicion, and odd thought patterns. Understanding these disorders helps in recognizing subtle signs of strange behaviors. Cluster

A's diverse manifestations, ranging from paranoid distrust to schizoid detachment, points out the intricate landscape of eccentricity in the realm of personality disorders.

Cluster B: Cluster B personality disorders are identified by emotional or erratic behavior. Borderline, Narcissistic, Antisocial, and Histrionic Personality Disorders are all part of this group. Individuals may struggle with volatile emotions, impulsive behavior, and difficulties forming stable relationships. This cluster sheds light on the tumultuous emotional terrain, from intense fear of being abandoned in Borderline Personality Disorder to arrogance in Narcissistic Personality Disorder. Understanding these dynamics is important for understanding the complexities of emotional and erratic behavior within the personality disorder spectrum.

Cluster C: Cluster C personality disorders are distinguished by anxious and nervous behavior. Obsessive-compulsive, Dependent, and Avoidant personality disorders are included in this cluster.

From the avoidance of social interactions in Avoidant Personality Disorder to the excessive need for reassurance in Dependent Personality Disorder and the rigid adherence to rules in Obsessive-Compulsive Personality Disorder, understanding these anxious behaviors is important for effective diagnosis and treatment.

Dependent Personality Disorder is in Cluster C.

CHAPTER ONE

Understanding DPD

Dependent Personality Disorder (DPD) is a complex mental health condition that falls under the Cluster C personality disorders category.

DPD, which is characterized by a pervasive and excessive need for others to take care of the individual, can have a significant impact on many aspects of an individual's life, ranging from personal relationships to professional growth. Exploring the nuances of this disorder is essential for developing empathy, providing effective support, and guiding individuals on the path to recovery.

Origins and Development

Dependent personality disorder often has its foundations in early life experiences. This disorder may develop as a result of childhood environments marked by inconsistent or overly protective parenting. The individual might internalize the idea that they can't manage life's obstacles on their own, which would encourage them to depend on other people for both practical and emotional support.

Effect on Day-To-Day Life

DPD affects many aspects of a person's life. Career growth can be impeded by individuals avoiding roles that require independent thinking in professional settings. The fear of abandonment can cause behaviors that strain relationships, which has a significant impact on personal relationships as well. It can be difficult to break the cycle of dependency that results from a persistent need for reassurance and support.

CHAPTER TWO

Signs and symptoms of DPD

For the purpose of early detection and intervention, it is important to fully understand the symptoms and signs of DPD. This chapter addresses the main symptoms associated to this disorder.

Some of these symptoms may include the following:

-Submissive Behavior: People living with DPD frequently display submissive behavior, constantly looking to others for approval and guidance. This may show up as a reluctance to express one's own opinions or act independently when making decisions.

-Making Decisions with the Help of Friends and Family: The consistent reliance on friends and family for decision-making is an obvious sign of DPD. Those affected may struggle to make even simple decisions without external help, prolonging a cycle of dependency.

-Needing Continuous Assurance: To reduce feelings of insecurity and self-doubt, individuals with DPD usually need constant reassurance from others. Even for everyday tasks, they might continually seek affirmation and validation.

-Easily Getting Hurt by Disapproval: Individuals with DPD are extremely sensitive to criticism or disapproval. Constructive feedback or perceived rejection can cause increased emotional distress as well as a deep fear of disappointing others.

-Feeling Isolated and Anxious When Alone: DPD is identified by a fear of being alone. Individuals may experience anxiety and nervousness when they are alone, causing them to avoid solitude.

-Fear of Rejection: A common symptom of DPD is a deep-seated fear of rejection. This fear can make it difficult to build healthy relationships and fuel a strong need to win people over in order to keep oneself from being abandoned.

-Being Extremely Sensitive to Criticism: Individuals with DPD may find it especially difficult to take criticism, even when it is constructive. Due to their increased sensitivity, they can react emotionally in a way that is out of proportion to the criticism they have received.

-Being Incapable of Being Alone: Individuals with DPD often find it difficult to be alone and seek constant companionship in an effort to prevent feelings of inferiority and loneliness. This reliance on other people for emotional support might thwart personal growth.

-Being Naive: Naivety is a common trait in individuals with DPD, as they may be overly trusting and easily influenced by others. As a result, they may be vulnerable to exploitation and manipulation.

-Fear of Abandonment: The fear of abandonment is perhaps the most significant fear associated with DPD. This fear can motivate people to go to great lengths to keep relationships intact, even if it requires forfeiting their own needs and desires.

Individuals with DPD who find themselves alone can experience a wide range of intense emotions and experiences. These could include:

Nervousness: Being alone often worsens the inherent nervousness that individuals with DPD may already experience in social situations. The lack of immediate external validation can cause anxiety, making solitude a difficult and uncomfortable experience.

Panic Attacks: For individuals with DPD, the prospect of being alone can cause panic attacks. The fear of abandonment, combined with the absence of a supportive presence, can lead to overwhelming anxiety, palpitations, and a sense of impending doom.

Fear: Individuals with DPD may experience a pervasive sense of fear in addition to their solitude. This fear stems not only from the fear of being alone, but also from the uncertainty of navigating life without constant guidance and support from others.

Hopelessness: For someone with DPD, alone time may worsen feelings of hopelessness. Individuals who struggle with the belief that they are unable to cope on their own may experience feelings of despair as a result of a lack of external reassurance.

Recognizing Dependent Personality Disorder symptoms is critical for timely intervention and effective treatment. By understanding these indicators, individuals, friends, and family can provide the necessary support and encourage those affected to seek professional help in order to promote independence and emotional stability.

CHAPTER THREE

Cognitive distortions of DPD

Dependent Personality Disorder (DPD) tends to be associated with specific cognitive distortions - thought patterns that contribute to the disorder's maintenance and aggravation. Individuals with DPD perceive themselves, others, and the world around them through these distortions. Understanding these cognitive distortions is vital for therapeutic interventions to be effective.

Here's a more in-depth look at the cognitive distortions linked to Dependent Personality Disorder:

1. Catastrophizing:

Description: People who have DPD may have catastrophic thinking, which is the tendency to imagine the worst case scenario. This distortion makes the fear of being left alone or abandoned more intense, which makes one worry excessively about possible bad outcomes.

Impact: Catastrophizing increases anxiety, which makes it difficult for people to carry out independent activities. Fear of disastrous consequences has the power to prevent people from making decisions and to keep them dependent on other people for comfort.

2. All-or-Nothing Thinking:

Description: This distortion occurs when one only perceives things in black and white, failing to see any gray areas or middle ground. Relationships may appear to be wholly accepting or entirely rejecting to people with DPD, leaving little opportunity for nuance.

Impact: An increased fear of abandonment may result from all-or-nothing thinking. Individuals may find it difficult to acknowledge the complexities in relationships, which makes it challenging for them to deal with the normal ups and downs without feeling strong emotional reactions.

3. Personalization:

Description: Attributing external occurrences to oneself, even in cases where there is no logical connection, is known as personalization. Individuals suffering from DPD might internalize external events, perceiving them as a reflection of their own inadequacy.

  Impact: This distortion heightens dependence on outside validation and leads to a distorted self-image. People may place an undue amount of blame on themselves for bad things that happen to them, which makes them feel even more powerless and dependent on other people.

4. Filtering:

Description: Selectively concentrating on a situation's negative aspects while ignoring its positive aspects is known as filtering. To reinforce their sense of dependence, individuals with DPD may ignore evidence of their own abilities or the support they receive.

  Impact: Individuals who selectively ignore good news could continue to have a skewed perception of their own skills and the amount of support that is available to them. This feeds the vicious cycle of low self-esteem and dependence on other people for validation.

5. Mind-Reading:

Description: Mind reading is the practice of making assumptions about other people's thoughts in the absence of concrete evidence. People with DPD might think that other people find them unworthy or burdensome, which makes them more anxious and afraid of being rejected.

Impact: Mind reading creates a self-fulfilling prophecy because people change how they behave based on erroneous beliefs about how others see them. Relationships may suffer as a result, and the demand for continuous assurance may increase.

6. Emotional Reasoning:

Description: Individuals who equate their emotions with reality are engaging in emotional reasoning. Individuals with DPD could think that their feelings of inadequacy are real, which would reinforce a distorted self-image.

Impact: Feelings of dependence and inadequacy are heightened by this distortion. It may be difficult for individuals to question the validity of their emotions, which hinders efforts to build autonomy and self-confidence.

7. Overgeneralization:

Description: Making broad, sweeping assumptions based on limited data is known as overgeneralization. Individuals suffering from DPD could generalize bad relationship experiences to all future encounters, anticipating the same results.

Impact: Individuals tend to project unpleasant memories from the past onto new relationships, which leads to overgeneralization and the widespread fear of abandonment. This distortion encourages dependency and hinders the development of positive relationships.

In order to effectively treat patients with Dependent Personality Disorder, it is imperative to recognize and address these cognitive distortions. For the purpose of promoting healthier viewpoints, increased autonomy, and self-confidence, cognitive-behavioral therapy (CBT) is frequently used to help individuals in recognizing and challenging these erroneous thought patterns.

CHAPTER FOUR

Distinguishing DPD from Other Personality Disorders

Personality disorders are a group of mental health conditions characterized by persistent patterns of behavior, cognition, and inner experience that deviate significantly from cultural norms. Differentiating these disorders is extremely important for accurate diagnosis and treatment. Dependent Personality Disorder (DPD) stands out among them, with distinct characteristics that sets it apart.

Below is an overview of the differences between Dependent Personality Disorder (DPD) and other Personality Disorders:

1. **Dependent vs. Borderline Personality Disorder (BPD):** While both disorders are characterized by a fear of abandonment, individuals with BPD may exhibit more impulsive behaviors, intense and unstable relationships, and a distorted self-image.

DPD focuses more on dependency and a need for support, whereas BPD is defined by emotional dysregulation.

2. **Dependent Personality Disorder (DPD) vs. Avoidant Personality Disorder (AvPD):** Dependent Personality Disorder emphasizes the need for others to take control, whereas Avoidant Personality Disorder is marked by social inhibition, feelings of inadequacy, and hypersensitivity to negative evaluation.

DPD involves a fear of being alone, whereas AvPD is concerned with the fear of rejection and criticism.

3. **Dependent vs. Narcissistic Personality Disorder (NPD):** While Narcissistic Personality Disorder is marked by a grandiose sense of self-importance and a lack of empathy, Dependent Personality Disorder is characterized by a lack of self-confidence and an insatiable need for reassurance.

Individuals with DPD are more likely to credit their accomplishments to others rather than claiming personal achievement.

4. **Dependent vs. Obsessive-Compulsive Personality Disorder (OCPD):** Although both disorders involve perfectionism, OCPD is distinguished by an obsession with orderliness and control.

DPD individuals seek support and reassurance, whereas OCPD people want to keep control of their environment.

Treatment and Outlook

Psychotherapy, particularly cognitive-behavioral therapy (CBT), tends to be effective in treating Dependent Personality Disorder. The therapeutic focus is on developing self-esteem, promoting autonomy, and developing more positive interpersonal relationships. If symptoms such as anxiety or depression are present, medication may be used to treat them.

Finally, while Dependent Personality Disorder shares certain features with other personality disorders, its distinguishing features are the pervasive need for support and the fear of abandonment. Recognizing these characteristics is essential for making an

accurate diagnosis and developing targeted
therapeutic interventions.

Co-occurring Disorders to Consider

Co-occurring disorders, also known as comorbidities, complicate understanding and treatment of mental health conditions. Individuals with Dependent Personality Disorder (DPD) are no exception, as they may also struggle with other co-occurring disorders that impact their overall well-being. Investigating these interconnected issues is critical for effective diagnosis and intervention.

The co-occurring disorders to look out for may include the following:

- **Dependent Personality Disorder (DPD):** The disorder is defined by an excessive need to be cared for, which leads to submissive and clinging behavior. Individuals with DPD often have difficulty with making everyday decisions in the absence of excessive advice and reassurance from others. This dependency can intertwine with a variety of co-occurring disorders, complicating the challenges for both the individual and mental health professionals.

-Generalized Anxiety Disorder (GAD): This is a common co-occurring disorder with DPD. DPD's constant need for reassurance and fear of making decisions aligns with GAD's persistent and excessive worry. These individuals may experience increased anxiety, anticipating negative outcomes even in routine situations. The combined impact of DPD and GAD can result in a cycle of dependence and anxiety that must be carefully considered in treatment planning.

-Major Depressive Disorder (MDD): This is another notable co-occurring disorder. When dependent individuals see themselves as burdensome or incapable, they may feel a profound sense of worthlessness and hopelessness. The core symptoms of MDD, such as persistent sadness and loss of interest, can aggravate the emotional difficulties that those with DPD face. Addressing both conditions at the same time is important for fostering a comprehensive therapeutic approach.

-Social Anxiety Disorder (SAD): Individuals with Dependent Personality Disorder are also prone to Social Anxiety Disorder. The fear of negative evaluation and social rejection that is commonly associated with SAD corresponds to DPD's desire for approval and acceptance. This overlap can manifest in avoidance of social situations or extreme discomfort when interacting with others, hindering personal and social development even further.

-Substance Use Disorder (SUD): This disorder frequently co-occur with Dependent Personality Disorder, adding to the complication. Individuals suffering from DPD may turn to substances to cope with their emotional dependence and insecurities.

The symptoms of DPD can be concealed by substance usage, which makes it challenging to diagnose and treat the underlying personality disorder.

It is critical for a successful recovery process to treat both by conditions at the same time.

-Borderline Personality Disorder (BPD): Another co-occurring disorder that can complicate the clinical picture is Borderline Personality Disorder (BPD). DPD and BPD both cause difficulties in interpersonal relationships, but they manifest in different ways. While DPD is distinguished by a submissive and clinging demeanor, BPD is distinguished by intense and volatile relationships. The interplay between these disorders necessitates a nuanced approach, taking into account the distinct challenges that each presents.

-Attention-Deficit/Hyperactivity Disorder (ADHD): In the context of co-occurring disorders with DPD, Attention-Deficit/Hyperactivity Disorder is also relevant. The impulsivity and inattention characteristic of ADHD may exacerbate the difficulty in making decisions and the need for external guidance in DPD. A comprehensive treatment plan must balance the management of attention-related symptoms with the core features of DPD.

-Post-Traumatic Stress Disorder (PTSD): It is important to recognize the potential impact of trauma, particularly Post-Traumatic Stress Disorder, in the realm of co-occurring disorders. Traumatic events can contribute to the development of both DPD and PTSD, resulting in a complicated interplay of symptoms. Addressing the trauma history is critical to effectively understanding and treating co-occurring disorders.

A multidisciplinary team is required for a comprehensive treatment approach for co-occurring disorders involving DPD. Individuals with DPD can benefit from psychotherapy, particularly cognitive-behavioral therapy (CBT), which can help them challenge and modify maladaptive thought patterns and behaviors. Medication management may be considered, particularly if the co-occurring disorder includes mood or anxiety symptoms.

Peer interventions and support groups play an essential role in addressing the social and interpersonal aspects of DPD. Creating a supportive community can help to combat the isolating tendencies of DPD and co-occurring disorders. In addition, stress-reduction techniques such as mindfulness and relaxation exercises can help with overall symptom management.

In conclusion, understanding and treating co-occurring disorders in the context of Dependent Personality Disorder is critical for comprehensive and effective treatment. Due to the complex interplay between DPD and other mental health conditions, a tailored and holistic approach combining psychotherapy, medication management, and supportive interventions is required. Mental health professionals can help individuals with DPD navigate a path to better health and independence by acknowledging and managing co-occurring disorders.

CHAPTER FIVE

Risk Factors Contributing to Dependent Personality Disorder

Dependent Personality Disorder (DPD) is a complex mental health condition that is influenced by a number of factors. Understanding the risk factors for the development of Dependent Personality Disorder is critical for early detection, prevention, and effective intervention. Here's a more in-depth look at the risk factors:

1. Early Attachment Experiences:

Description: The quality of early attachment experiences influences the development of personality traits such as dependency. Individuals who receive inconsistent care, are neglected, or have overly controlling caregivers may be at a higher risk of developing DPD.

Impact: Insecure attachment can lead to a deep fear of abandonment and excessive dependence on others for emotional security. These early relationships shape individual's expectations of relationships, shaping their interpersonal dynamics throughout their lives.

2. Childhood Adversity and Trauma:

Description: DPD can be worsened by traumatic events or adverse childhood experiences, such as physical or emotional abuse. Trauma can interfere with the development of healthy coping mechanisms and increase the need for external assistance.

Impact: Adversity in childhood can contribute to the development of maladaptive coping strategies, such as excessive dependence on others. DPD may develop as a way for trauma survivors to seek safety and stability in relationships.

3. Overprotective Parenting

Description: Overprotective or controlling parents may unintentionally contribute to the development of DPD. Overprotective parenting prevents children from developing autonomy and decision-making skills.

Impact: Individuals raised in overly protective environments may struggle with independent decision-making and experience increased anxiety when faced with making decisions on their own. This may play a role in the dependent patterns observed in DPD.

4. Genetic and Biological Factors:

Description: Evidence suggests a genetic component in the development of personality disorders, including DPD. Temperament and personality traits that increase vulnerability to the disorder may be influenced by genetic factors.

Impact: While genetics alone do not cause DPD, they may influence an individual's proclivity for certain personality traits associated with dependence. To shape personality development, environmental factors interact with genetic predispositions.

5. Personality traits:

Description: Certain personality traits, such as high neuroticism or low self-esteem, may be risk factors for DPD. Individuals who exhibit these characteristics may be predisposed to developing maladaptive dependency patterns.

Impact: Personality traits contribute to an individual's overall vulnerability to the development of specific personality disorders. For example, increased sensitivity to rejection may contribute to DPD's intense fear of abandonment.

6. Social and Cultural Factors:

Description: Social and cultural expectations can have an impact on the development of personality disorders. Cultural norms that favor collectivism over individualism may contribute to the development of dependent characteristics.

Impact: Cultural and societal expectations about interpersonal relationships can influence people's beliefs and behaviors. Individuals in cultures that value interdependence may be more prone to developing dependent patterns in order to meet societal expectations.

7. Co-occurring Mental Health Conditions:

Description: Individuals who have co-occurring mental health conditions, such as anxiety or mood disorders, may be more likely to develop DPD. These conditions' symptoms can contribute to an increased need for external support and reassurance.

Impact: Mental health issues frequently interact and influence one another. Comorbid conditions must be addressed in the treatment of DPD because the presence of symptoms from other disorders may exacerbate dependency patterns.

8. Major Life Events:

Description: Significant life events, such as the death of a loved one or major life transitions, may trigger or worsen DPD symptoms. These occurrences could increase the need for external support and reassurance.

Impact: Individuals going through major life changes may seek support from others during times of stress. As a way to cope with the emotional challenges associated with significant life events, dependency patterns may emerge or intensify.

Understanding these risk factors can help mental health professionals, caregivers, and individuals themselves. These risk factors can be mitigated by early intervention, supportive environments, and targeted therapeutic approaches, which promote healthier patterns of independence and self-reliance.

CHAPTER SIX

Diagnosis and Treatment for DPD

Dependent Personality Disorder (DPD) is a mental health condition characterized by an overwhelming desire to be cared for. Individuals with DPD often have difficulty making decisions, require constant reassurance, and are afraid of being abandoned. DPD diagnosis and treatment require a holistic approach to understanding and addressing the underlying issues that contribute to the disorder.

DEPENDENT PERSONALITY DISORDER DIAGNOSIS

DPD must be diagnosed by a qualified mental health professional after a careful and thorough assessment. The following elements are typically included in the process:

1. Clinical Interview: A clinical interview is conducted by a mental health professional to gather information about the individual's symptoms, personal history, and current life circumstances. This helps in understanding the context in which the symptoms developed.

2. Diagnostic Criteria: The Diagnostic and Statistical Manual of Mental Disorders (DSM-5) specifies diagnostic criteria for Dependent Personality Disorder. The clinician determines whether the person meets these criteria, which include excessive reliance on others, difficulty making decisions without reassurance, and a strong fear of abandonment.

3. Rule out any other conditions: Other mental health conditions that may present with similar symptoms must be ruled out. DPD may coexist with other disorders such as anxiety or mood disorders. A thorough examination assists in distinguishing between primary and secondary symptoms.

4. Psychological Testing: Psychological tests and assessments may be used to gain a better understanding of an individual's cognitive and emotional functioning. These tests can help to support the diagnosis and guide treatment planning by providing additional information.

5. Collateral Information: Information from secondary sources, such as family members or close friends, may be considered to gain a more complete understanding of the individual's behavior and relationships. This can provide valuable insight into how DPD affects various aspects of a person's life.

HOW TO TREAT DEPENDENT PERSONALITY DISORDER

Following a DPD diagnosis, treatment aims to address the core symptoms, improve overall functioning, and promote independence. In the treatment of Dependent Personality Disorder, the following therapeutic approaches are commonly used:

1. Psychotherapy: CBT is a popular treatment option for DPD. It focuses on identifying and challenging maladaptive thought patterns and behaviors related to addiction. Individuals learn to recognize and correct distorted thinking, make independent decisions, and increase their self-esteem.

2. Psychodynamic Therapy: Unconscious patterns and conflicts that contribute to dependent behaviors are investigated in psychodynamic therapy. It seeks to increase self-awareness, identify underlying issues, and promote healthier coping mechanisms. The therapeutic relationship is critical in dealing with attachment issues and fostering independence.

3. Mindfulness-Based Interventions: Mindfulness practices such as meditation and mindful awareness can help people with DPD. These practices help people stay in the present moment, reduce anxiety about the future, and cultivate a sense of inner stability.

4. Social Skills Training: This type of training focuses on developing interpersonal skills and assertiveness. Individuals with DPD frequently have difficulty expressing their needs and desires. Social skills training aids in the development of effective communication strategies and reduces reliance on others for decision-making.

5. Gradual Exposure: Gradual exposure entails gradually confronting and overcoming fears associated with independence. Therapists work with individuals to create a progression of increasingly difficult situations. This methodical approach allows individuals to gradually gain confidence and autonomy.

6. Medication: While no specific medication for DPD is approved, pharmacotherapy may be considered to address co-occurring symptoms such as anxiety or depression. Under the supervision of a psychiatrist, antidepressant or anti-anxiety medications may be prescribed.

7. Supportive Group Therapy: Group therapy allows individuals with DPD to connect with others who are going through similar situations. It provides a safe environment in which to practice social skills, receive feedback, and gain insights from various perspectives.

8. Family Therapy: Involving family members in therapy can be beneficial, particularly if family dynamics contribute to or are influenced by DPD. Family therapy focuses on communication patterns, boundaries, and ways to assist individuals in developing independence.

9. Goal Setting and Achievement: Goal-setting is an essential component of DPD treatment. Setting realistic and achievable goals collaboratively helps individuals develop a sense of accomplishment and self-efficacy. Therapists direct the process, ensuring that goals are consistent with the individual's values and goals.

Challenges in Treatment

1. Resistance Independence: to Individuals with DPD may initially resist efforts to promote independence out of fear of being abandoned. Therapists gradually establish trust and foster a supportive environment in which autonomy is encouraged.

2. Examining Underlying Issues: It can be difficult to identify and address underlying issues such as attachment patterns and past traumas. Therapists navigate these delicate waters in order to promote healing and understanding.

3. Maintaining Motivation: It is critical to maintain motivation for change. Therapists use motivational enhancement strategies, emphasizing the advantages of increased independence and quality of life.

4. Addressing Co-Occurring Conditions: Many people with DPD have co-occurring mental health issues. To achieve comprehensive and long-term improvements, effective treatment must address these conditions in addition to DPD.

In conclusion, Dependent Personality Disorder is a complicated disorder that requires a multifaceted approach to diagnosis and treatment. Positive outcomes can be achieved through a combination of psychotherapy, mindfulness practices, social skills training, and family involvement. Individuals are empowered to make independent decisions, build self-confidence, and cultivate healthy relationships as part of the therapeutic process. Individuals with DPD can achieve greater autonomy and a more fulfilling life through collaborative efforts between them and their mental health professionals.

CHAPTER SEVEN

Coping Strategies

Coping with Dependent Personality Disorder requires numerous strategies that address the core issues of excessive dependence and the resulting fear of independence.

Individuals with DPD often have trouble with decision-making, relationship maintenance and promoting independence. Implementing effective coping strategies can improve their quality of life and promote personal development.

Here, we will explore the various coping mechanisms that are tailored to the specific needs of individuals with Dependent Personality Disorder.

The following coping mechanisms may be useful if you live with dependent personality disorder:

- **Start doing things alone:** It's helpful to gradually challenge yourself to do things alone, starting with easier challenges and progressing to more difficult ones. For example, you could begin by going grocery shopping alone and work your way up to eating a meal at a restaurant by yourself.

- **Engage in physical activities:** It can be beneficial to start working out and to push yourself to do a little bit more each day. Knowing that you can push your physical and mental limits can make you feel stronger and more capable.

- **Work on becoming independent:** Examine your relationships with loved ones and identify ways in which you are dependent on others. Start learning to be independent without their assistance, one step at a time. Try taking over one task that someone else does for you every week or month.

- **Start trusting yourself:** Begin to trust yourself by paying attention to your thoughts, feelings, and instincts. Before seeking other people's opinions when making a decision, think about them and pay attention to how you feel. Trust your instincts and have confidence in your ability to handle any outcome.

- **Therapy and Counseling:** Engaging in psychotherapy, particularly cognitive-behavioral therapy (CBT) or dialectical behavior therapy (DBT), can be extremely beneficial. These therapies assist individuals in identifying and changing negative thought patterns as well as developing healthier coping mechanisms.

- **Examine your need for approval:** Remember that liking approval and enjoying it is not the same as needing others' approval to function.

- **Assertiveness Training:** Learning to express your needs and opinions assertively is essential in overcoming dependency. This entails learning effective communication skills in order to clearly convey your thoughts and feelings without being passive or aggressive.

- **Establish Boundaries:** It is critical to establish and maintain healthy boundaries. Individuals with DPD frequently struggle with setting boundaries, so learning to say no, express personal limits, and prioritize self-care is essential.

- **Develop Effective Problem-Solving Skills:** Learning effective problem-solving skills can boost autonomy. This entails breaking down problems into manageable steps, evaluating alternatives, and implementing solutions.

- **Medication Management:** In some cases, medication may be prescribed to treat symptoms of anxiety or depression associated with DPD. Consultation with a psychiatrist can help determine whether medication is a viable option.

It's important to remember that coping strategies differ from person to person, and a tailored approach is often the most effective. Seeking professional advice and support is essential for developing a comprehensive plan for managing Dependent Personality Disorder.

CHAPTER EIGHT

Building Awareness

Developing self-awareness is an important part of the therapeutic process for people with DPD. This involves identifying the triggers that contribute to dependent behavior, such as:

Stressful life event: Life events that are stressful may trigger or worsen dependent behaviors. Recognizing these triggers involves recognizing situations where stress increases the need for reassurance or support. This could include significant life changes, work-related stress, or personal difficulties.

Conflict and disagreement: Conflicts and disagreement can serve as catalysts for dependent behavior. Individuals with DPD may struggle to assert themselves or express different points of view in order to avoid rejection or abandonment. Recognizing this trigger involves reflecting on reactions during conflicts.

Perceived Rejection: DPD is marked by a fear of rejection, and perceived rejection can trigger dependent behaviors. Recognizing this trigger involves understanding how sensitivity to perceived rejection influences thoughts and actions, such as seeking constant validation to alleviate rejection feelings.

Change in Relationships: Relationship changes, such as a friend withdrawing or a partner asserting independence, can act as triggers. Recognizing this involves being aware of emotional responses to changes in relationships, as well as the subsequent desire for more reassurance.

Loneliness or Isolation: Individuals seeking connection and support may become dependent when they are isolated or lonely. Recognizing this trigger involves recognizing moments of heightened dependence during periods of isolation and understanding the role of these behaviors in coping with loneliness.

Decision-Making and Uncertainty: Uncertainty or the need to make independent decisions can be powerful motivators for dependent behavior.

Recognizing this involves acknowledging the discomfort or anxiety associated with making decisions and relying on others for guidance as a result.

Developing Self-Awareness Strategies

Mindfulness Practices:

Meditation and mindful awareness, for example, can help individuals with DPD become more aware of their thoughts and emotions. Mindfulness promotes the ability to observe patterns of dependence without immediately passing judgment, thereby increasing self-awareness.

Journaling:

Individuals who keep a journal can keep track of their thoughts, emotions, and behaviors. Reflecting on journal entries on a regular basis can reveal patterns of dependence and assist in identifying triggers. By providing a tangible record of experiences, this process promotes self-awareness.

Therapeutic Interventions:

Psychotherapy, particularly cognitive-behavioral therapy (CBT) and psychodynamic therapy, is a prerequisite for self-awareness development. Therapists guide individuals in exploring patterns of dependence, identify triggers, and develop healthier coping mechanisms.

Self-reflection Exercises:

Self-reflection exercises, such as writing about personal strengths and challenges, can help individuals become more self-aware. Individuals are able to examine how patterns of dependency affect their lives and identify opportunities for growth and change.

Support Groups:

Individuals with DPD who participate in support groups have the opportunity to share their experiences and learn from others who are facing similar challenges. As individuals reflect on shared experiences and perspectives, group discussions promote self-awareness.

Gradual Exposure:

Individuals can confront and understand their reactions when they are gradually exposed to situations that trigger dependent behaviors.

Therapists assist patients in gradually confronting triggers, developing resilience, and developing more adaptive responses.

In conclusion, self-awareness development in Dependent Personality Disorder involves a thorough examination of unhealthy patterns of dependence as well as the identification of triggers that contribute to dependent behavior. Individuals can gain valuable insights into their thoughts, emotions, and behaviors through mindfulness practices, journaling, therapeutic interventions, self-reflection exercises, and support groups. Self-awareness is the foundation for personal growth, allowing individuals with DPD to navigate relationships more independently and develop a stronger sense of self. Individuals who become more aware of their patterns and triggers can work to foster healthier relationships and improve their overall well-being.

CHAPTER NINE

Developing Self-Esteem

Dependent Personality Disorder (DPD) can have a significant impact on self-esteem, so it is important to work on developing a positive self-image. This chapter explores effective strategies, with a focus on recognizing personal strengths and setting and achieving small goals.

Recognizing Personal Strengths

-Self-Reflection: Start by engaging in regular self-reflection. Recognize and appreciate your distinct qualities, talents, and accomplishments. This process helps in the development of a positive self-image.

-Strengths Assessment: Conduct a strengths assessment to identify areas where you excel. Recognizing one's strengths, whether in interpersonal skills, creativity, or problem-solving abilities, contributes to a more robust sense of self.

-**Affirmations:** Integrate positive affirmations into your daily routine. Repeat phrases like "I am resilient and capable, facing challenges with courage and determination."

 This practice has the potential to reshape negative thought patterns over time.

Setting and Achieving Small Goals

1. SMART Objectives:

Define specific goals, such as "improve time management skills."

Set metrics, such as "Complete tasks within specified timeframes."

Achievable: Make sure your goals are realistic and achievable.

Relevant: Align your goals with your personal values and long-term goals.

Time-bound: Establish deadlines for completing each goal.

2. Start Small:

Begin with small, easily attainable goals. Success in these initial endeavors builds confidence and motivates individuals to take on more difficult tasks in the future.

The first goal is to finish a daily task without seeking excessive reassurance.

Make an independent decision and then reflect on the positive outcome.

3. Celebrate Achievements:

3. Celebrate Achievements: Every accomplishment, no matter how big or small, should be celebrated. Recognizing and acknowledging accomplishments, no matter how minor, helps to reinforce a positive self-image.

Acknowledge even the smallest victories to reinforce positive behavior.

Completing a task without constantly seeking validation is a significant accomplishment.

4. Gradual Progression: As self-esteem grows, gradually increase the complexity of goals. This step-by-step approach prevents overwhelming feelings and maintains a steady rate of personal development.

Increase the complexity of goals gradually.

For instance, progress from making small independent decisions to taking the lead in a group project.

Building self-esteem in individuals with Dependent Personality Disorder requires a multifaceted approach. Individuals can cultivate a positive self-image and navigate life's challenges with increased confidence and resilience by recognizing personal strengths, setting SMART goals, and incorporating additional strategies. Remember that while progress may be slow, each step forward is a victory worth celebrating.

CHAPTER TEN

Becoming Independent

It usually takes a combination of self-reflection, therapeutic interventions, and practical lifestyle changes to overcome Dependent Personality Disorder (DPD) and develop independence.

This is a thorough guide to help you in becoming independent:

1. Acknowledgment and Acceptance: Admit that being dependent is difficult.

Recognize that change comes gradually, and practice patience with yourself.

2. Self-Exploration:

Identify dependency triggers

Recognize the relationships or situations that lead to dependency.

Recognize the underlying feelings and thoughts that come with dependency.

3. Examine Your Personal Values:

Define your beliefs and values on your own, without reference to other people.

Try to live your life in accordance with these values by reflecting on what matters most to you.

4. Developing Assertiveness:

To confidently voice your needs and opinions, learn assertiveness techniques.

Practice saying "no" when it's necessary and without guilt.

5. Taking on Responsibilities:

Take on new duties in various aspects of life one by one.

Strive to be an independent decision-maker.

6. Mindfulness and Stress management:

Practice deep breathing exercises and mindfulness meditation.

To deal with anxiety, practice stress reduction strategies.

7. Social support and healthy relationships:

Nurture healthy relationships that enhance your independence.

Surround yourself with people who support your personal development.

Join support groups to make connections with people going through similar struggles.

Discuss your experiences and gain insight from one another's journeys.

8. Celebrate your independence and reflect on your progress:

Assess your independence progress on a regular basis.

Celebrate your achievements and major milestones.

9. Professional Guidance:

To track progress, follow up with mental health specialists on a regular basis.

Adjust therapeutic interventions as needed.

10. Healthy Lifestyle choices:

Make physical well-being a priority through regular exercise and a balanced diet.

Make sure you get enough sleep to maintain emotional stability.

11. Maintain Awareness and Adapt:

 Assess tactics frequently and make necessary adjustments.

Be aware of possible failures and take lessons from them.

Remember that overcoming Dependent Personality Disorder is a journey that requires commitment and self-compassion. Gradually implementing these strategies can lead to increased independence and overall well-being.

CHAPTER ELEVEN

Mindfulness Exercises

Mindfulness exercises can be effective tools for individuals dealing with Dependent Personality Disorder (DPD).

Here are six mindfulness exercises to help you overcome Dependent Personality Disorder:

1. Breathe Awareness:

Breath awareness is a simple yet effective mindfulness exercise that can help with the treatment of Dependent Personality Disorder.

Follow these steps:

Choose a quiet and comfortable spot where you will not be disturbed.

Sit or lie down in a position that is comfortable for you. If you're sitting, make sure your back is straight and your hands are resting comfortably.

If comfortable, close your eyes to reduce external distractions.

Pay attention to your breath. Take note of the sensation of each inhale and exhale.

Feel the gentle expansion and contraction of your abdomen or the rise and fall of your chest.

Observe your breath without judgment. If your thoughts wander, softly return them to your breathing.

Count breath cycles by slowly inhaling to the count of four and slowly exhaling to the count of six.

Adjust the count to feel comfortable, making sure the exhale is longer than the inhale.

Pay attention to each breath, taking note of the sensation of each breathe in and breathe out.

If distracting thoughts arise, acknowledge them and return your focus to your breath.

Now imagine releasing tension and stress with each exhale as you breathe out.

Allow your body to gradually relax with each breath.

Engage senses by observing the cool sensation of inhaling and the warm sensation of exhaling.

Be unattached to any smells or sounds in your environment.

After a few minutes, gradually return your attention to your surroundings.

Open your eyes if you had them closed.

This breath awareness exercise encourages calm and presence. Regular practice can benefit individuals suffering from Dependent Personality Disorder by increasing self-awareness, decreasing anxiety, and cultivating a greater sense of inner stability. Consistency is essential, so try to incorporate this exercise into your daily routine for the best results.

2. Body Scan Meditation:

This is a mindfulness exercise that promotes self-awareness and relaxation. It can be especially helpful for individuals overcoming Dependent Personality Disorder.

Follow these steps:

Lie down on your back or sit in a relaxed and comfortable position.

If you're comfortable, close your eyes to focus more on bodily sensations.

To start, take a few deep breaths to center yourself. Exhale slowly through your mouth and inhale slowly through your nose.

Focus your attention on your toes. Take note of any sensations, such as tension or warmth. If you feel any tension, exhale slowly and consciously.

Slowly shift your attention to the soles of your feet. Feel the connection to the earth. Observe any sensations without passing judgment.

Move your attention slowly up your body, scanning each part in turn—ankles, calves, knees, thighs, and so on.

Recognize any sensations, and if you notice any areas of tension, breathe into them to allow them to relax.

As you breathe, pay attention to your abdominal area. Feel the rise and fall with every breath.

As you move up to your chest, notice the gentle expansion and contraction.

Bring your attention to your fingers, hands, forearms, and upper arms.

As you exhale, let go of any tension.

Next, scan your neck and throat, then move on to your face and head.

Be aware of any sensations and consciously relax your facial muscles.

After completing the scan, take a few moments to focus on your entire body.

Feel the sense of connection and relaxation throughout your entire body.

Gradually return to a more active state when you are ready.

Wiggle your fingers and toes, and if your eyes are closed, open them.

Body scan meditation on a regular basis can help anyone suffering from Dependent Personality Disorder develop a heightened sense of bodily awareness, release tension, and cultivate a stronger connection with themselves. In order to reap long-term benefits, incorporate this exercise into your daily routine.

3. Mindful walking exercise:

Mindful walking is a grounding exercise that may help in the treatment of Dependent Personality Disorder by increasing awareness of the present moment.

Follow these steps:

Choose a quiet and safe area to walk. Depending on your preferences, it could be indoors or outdoors.

Start by standing still and breathing deeply. Concentrate on the present moment.

For your walk, set a mindful intention. "I will, for example, be fully present and aware of each step."

Start walking at a slower than usual pace. With each step, pay attention to how your body moves.

Pay attention to your feet's sensations as they lift off, move through the air, and make contact with the ground.

Be Present. Use all of your senses. Take note of the air temperature, the sounds around you, and any smells or textures you come across.

Take each step with purpose and awareness. Feel your heel touching the ground, your foot rolling, and your toes pushing off.

Avoid distractions by putting away electronic devices and try to keep distractions to a minimum. This is a time for intense concentration.

Increase the duration and depth of your meditation practice over time. Incorporate this meditation into your daily routine and see how it goes.

End with Gratitude. Take a few deep breaths to signal the end of the meditation. Express gratitude for the practice and the positive energy you've created.

Loving-kindness Meditation can be a life-changing practice for individuals suffering from Dependent Personality Disorder. It fosters a sense of inner strength and autonomy by encouraging self-love, compassion, and the ability to extend kindness to others. Regularly adding this meditation into your routine can help you feel better emotionally.

4. Gratitude journaling:

Gratitude journaling is a wonderful practice that can help individuals overcome Dependent Personality Disorder by refocusing their attention on the positive aspects of their lives.

For a gratitude journaling exercise, follow these steps:

Choose a journal specifically for your gratitude practice. Depending on your preferences, it could be a physical notebook or a digital platform.

Set aside time each day for your gratitude practice. This could be in the morning, before bedtime, or at a quiet time during the day.

Think about three things for which you are grateful. These can be simple or profound, and they can be about your personal life, relationships, accomplishments, or the world around you.

Be as specific as possible in your entries. Instead of making a broad statement like "I'm grateful for my family," focus on a specific interaction or aspect that brings you joy.

Explain why you are grateful for each gratitude entry. This strengthens your bond with the positive experiences.

Include aspects of personal growth or self-discovery that contribute to your journey of dependency recovery.

Review the past entries periodically. Reflect on how your perspective has shifted and the positive changes you've experienced.

Use gratitude journaling to combat negative thoughts. When faced with adversity, think about what you can still be grateful for.

Celebrate small victories and accomplishments. Recognize your progress, no matter how little.

If comfortable, share positive experiences from your gratitude journal with trusted friends or family. This can help to strengthen social bonds.

Give your gratitude practice time to adapt and evolve. Feel free to add drawings, quotes, or other elements to personalize your journal.

Consistency is important. Therefore, make gratitude journaling a regular part of your routine. The benefits tend to be realized through consistent practice.

Gratitude journaling can help you shift your focus to the positive aspects of life, cultivating an abundance and appreciation mindset. This practice can lead to increased resilience and a more positive outlook over time, helping in the process of overcoming Dependent Personality Disorder.

5. Thought-surfing exercise:

Thought-surfing is a mindfulness exercise that involves observing your thoughts without becoming entangled in them. Individuals overcoming Dependent Personality Disorder may benefit from this practice.

Follow these steps:

Choose a quiet and comfortable space where you can sit or lie down without being distracted.

Close your eyes if it helps you focus. Take a few deep breaths to ground yourself in the current moment.

Picture your thoughts as ocean waves. Observe how they naturally rise and fall.

Start by observing your thoughts objectively. Allow them to come and go like waves on the ocean's surface.

As the thoughts arise, label them simply without engaging with the content. For example, "planning," "worrying," or "remembering."

Maintain detachment by keeping your thoughts separate from you. You are the observer, not the content of the thought.

Acknowledge the fleeting nature of each thought. Recognize that, like waves, thoughts naturally dissipate.

If your mind becomes too focused on one thought, gently bring your attention back to your breath. Stay in the present moment by focusing on your breathing.

Gradually broaden your awareness to include bodily sensations and your surroundings. Feel your breathing, the temperature of the room, and any sounds.

Practice letting go if you notice yourself becoming emotionally attached to a thought. Imagine the thought to be a wave receding into the vast ocean.

If your mind becomes active again, resume your thought-surfing practice. Repetition is necessary to maintain a state of mindful observation.

When you're done with the exercise, take a few moments to reflect on it. Take note of any changes in your awareness or emotional state.

Thought-surfing assists individuals suffering from Dependent Personality Disorder in developing a mindful and non-reactive approach to their thoughts. This practice can contribute to a greater sense of mental freedom and autonomy by observing thoughts without being swept away by them. Over time, consistent practice will improve the effectiveness of thought-surfing.

6. Mindful listening:

Mindful listening is an excellent exercise for individuals dealing with Dependent Personality Disorder. This exercise promotes present-moment awareness and improves communication skills.

Follow these steps:

Choose a quiet location where you can concentrate without distractions. Depending on your preferences, this could be done indoors or outdoors.

Identify a sound source to concentrate on. It could be a speaker's voice, ambient sounds, or even soothing music.

Sit or stand comfortably, with your body relaxed. Maintain a straight back and comfortable hand position while seated.

Close your eyes to reduce visual distractions.

Focus your attention on the selected sound source. If someone is speaking, pay attention to what they are saying without becoming distracted by your own thoughts.

Observe the sounds unbiased. Allow yourself to be free of any preconceived notions or assumptions.

Practice deep listening. Pay attention not only to the words, but also to the tone, pace, and emotional undertones.

If you're having a conversation, resist the urge to respond right away. Allow for a short pause before responding.

If your thoughts begin to wander, gently bring them back to the sounds. To stay present, use your breath as an anchor.

Gradually broaden your awareness to include additional environmental sounds. Take note of subtle details you may not have noticed before.

When listening to someone speak, exercise empathy. Try to understand their point of view and emotions.

Express your appreciation for the sounds around you. Recognize the depth and breadth of the auditory experience.

When you're done with the exercise, pause for a few moments to reflect on your experience. Take note of any changes in your awareness or emotional state.

Mindful listening can help you connect with others, communicate effectively, and reduce your reliance on external validation. Regular practice will help to strengthen these skills over time, which will aid in your journey to overcome Dependent Personality Disorder.

CHAPTER TWELVE

Monitoring Progress

A Path of Reflection and Adaptation for Overcoming Dependent Personality Disorder

Dependent Personality Disorder (DPD) presents a unique set of challenges that require a thoughtful and adaptable approach to recovery. Monitoring progress is an important part of this journey, and it involves regular self-reflection and the ability to adjust strategies in response to feedback.

Individuals with DPD can more effectively navigate the path to independence and emotional well-being by incorporating these practices.

Continuous Self-Reflection:

On the road to recovery from DPD, regular self-reflection serves as a compass. It entails consciously examining one's thoughts, behaviors, and emotional responses. Individuals gain insights into patterns that may contribute to dependency and discover opportunities for growth through self-reflection.

Journaling is an effective method of self-reflection. Individuals who keep a journal can document their daily experiences, emotions, and challenges. Patterns and triggers can be identified by reviewing entries on a regular basis, providing valuable information for targeted intervention. This self-awareness serves as a foundation for comprehending dependencies and developing a proactive mindset.

Additionally, engaging in mindfulness practices promotes self-reflection. Mindful breathing and body scan meditations, for example, create a space for observing thoughts without judgment. This non-reactive awareness enables individuals to recognize dependencies as they arise, allowing them to respond more intentionally.

The journey to overcoming DPD is not a linear one, but rather an ongoing process that requires flexibility and adaptability. Adapting strategies in response to feedback is akin to recalibrating one's approach in response to the changing nature of personal challenges.

Self-reflection, therapy sessions, and interactions with supportive individuals can all provide feedback. In therapy, the professional's guidance and feedback become critical tools for understanding progress and areas that need to be addressed further. Individuals, in collaboration with their therapist, can refine and adapt strategies to effectively address specific challenges.

Social support networks are also important in providing feedback. Trusted friends or family members may provide insights into changes they notice, providing an external perspective to supplement self-reflection. Being open to this feedback and considering it with a growth mindset can lead to important changes in the recovery process.

When it comes to coping strategies, adaptability is crucial. What works at one stage of recovery may need to be modified as circumstances change. For example, if setting boundaries becomes a recurring challenge, it may be necessary to adjust communication strategies or seek additional support. The ability to recognize feedback, whether internal or external, fosters a proactive and resilient approach to overcoming DPD.

Finally, tracking progress toward overcoming Dependent Personality Disorder is a dynamic and personalized journey. Regular self-reflection acts as a compass, revealing personal patterns and triggers. Adapting strategies based on feedback, whether from therapy or social support networks, is essential for effectively adapting to changing challenges. Individuals with DPD can navigate their way to independence, resilience, and a more fulfilling life by embracing these practices.

CONCLUSION

Overcoming Dependent Personality Disorder (DPD) is a difficult but transformative journey that requires commitment, self-reflection, and an intricate approach. In this chapter, we'll look at key insights into the DPD recovery process, emphasizing the importance of self-awareness, therapeutic interventions, and a supportive environment.

The road to recovery from Dependent Personality Disorder begins with acknowledging the presence of the disorder and its impact on various aspects of one's life. Individuals with DPD frequently struggle with an excessive need for reassurance, an inability to make independent decisions, and a strong fear of abandonment. Recognizing these patterns is an important first step because it lays the groundwork for self-awareness.

Self-awareness is essential for overcoming DPD. Individuals can gain insights into their thought patterns, emotional responses, and interpersonal dynamics through introspection. Developing an acute awareness of one's own needs and fears enables targeted interventions and coping strategies. Individual and group therapy become essential tools in this process.

Therapeutic interventions are critical in the journey to recovery from DPD. CBT is particularly effective because it assists individuals in identifying and challenging maladaptive thoughts and behaviors. Individuals can gradually reduce their reliance on others for validation and decision-making by reshaping negative thought patterns and fostering healthier coping mechanisms.

In addition, psychodynamic therapy allows for a more in-depth exploration of underlying emotions and unresolved issues that contribute to DPD. Uncovering the causes of dependency allows individuals to address core issues, paving the way for long-term change. Individual sessions are supplemented by group therapy, which provides a supportive community in which individuals can share experiences, gain perspective, and practice interpersonal skills in a safe environment.

Another important aspect of overcoming DPD is developing and maintaining healthy relationships. Developing effective communication skills, establishing boundaries, and learning to assert one's needs all contribute to greater autonomy and less reliance on others.

 Friends and family play an important role in this process by providing encouragement and understanding during difficult times.

Also, developing self-esteem and a sense of self-worth are critical components of overcoming DPD. Activities that promote personal growth, goal setting and achievement, and celebrating individual accomplishments all contribute to a positive self-image. The grip of dependency loosens as individuals develop a stronger sense of self, allowing for more fulfilling and balanced relationships.

It is critical to recognize that overcoming DPD is not a straight-line process, and setbacks may occur. Patience and perseverance are essential virtues on this journey. Learning from setbacks, adjusting therapeutic approaches, and committing to personal growth all contribute to overall resilience.

In conclusion, overcoming Dependent Personality Disorder is a multifaceted journey that involves self-awareness, therapeutic interventions, and the development of healthy relationships. The process is time-consuming, but the benefits are profound: increased autonomy, self-esteem, and the ability to form more balanced and fulfilling connections with others. While the journey may be difficult, the positive impact on one's life makes it worthwhile.